MISTRESS OF THE WINDS

A STORY OF THE GARDENERS' UNIVERSE

story and art
par Michèle Laframboise

 ECHOFICTIONS

My warmest thanks to Frank Fournier
for his invaluable help !

Mistress of the Wind © 2022 Michèle Laframboise

Interior art @Michèle Laframboise

Cover Pic by Laframboise / Colors by Frank Fournier

Fonts design © Frank Fournier

Author portrait by Frédéric Gagnon

Interior author portrait by Gilles Gagnon

Published by Echofictions

ECHOFICTIONS

Mississauga, Ontario

ISBN 978-1-990824-07-4 Paperback

ISBN 978-1-990824-06-7 ebook

PART ONE

Wind is not an enemy...
but a playful friend!

ADALOU KHA NARRI! YOU WERE AT THE CLIFFS, AGAIN!

FLAUNTING YOUR UNPROTECTED BELLY IN PUBLIC!

WHAT DID YOU PICK UP?

THOSE RODS ARE MADE IN COMPOSITES

THEY ARE STILL IN GOOD SHAPE. I CAN BUILD MY OWN KITE WITH THEM!

YOUR ki--

BY THE GARDENER!

LEAVE THOSE FOLLIES TO THE IDLE OF THE HIGH SPIRAL!

YOU'LL SPEND THE MASTERMEAL IN YOUR ROOM!

YOU ARE TOO HARSH!

...

ADALOU?

MY FLOWER?

WHEN OUR CHILDHOOD RECEDES...

WE ALL GO THROUGH THIS TRIAL.

... OUR BELLIES BECOME SOFT.

HEY! GET OFF YOUR BASKET!

TAP TAP

NO.

YOUR FATHER CAME FROM A LOW HIRED-HANDS* FAMILY. HE WORKED HARD (ALONG WITH ME) TO REACH OUR CURRENT LEVEL OF PRESTIGE. SO HE CAN'T ACCEPT YOUR INDULGING IN "SILLY" PURSUITS, INSTEAD OF STUDYING.

* INDEBTED WORKERS

I HAD A TALK WITH YOUR BROTHER. TOMORROW, WE'RE GOING TO THE CRAFT FAIR. IT WILL BE A CHANGE, AND...

WE MIGHT EVEN GET TO SEE CUTE ACROBATS!

CRRR... CRRR...

FWIP!

ACROBATS?

Strambone 2011

PART TWO

* TEMPORAL UNIT, ABOUT ONE MINUTE AND A HALF

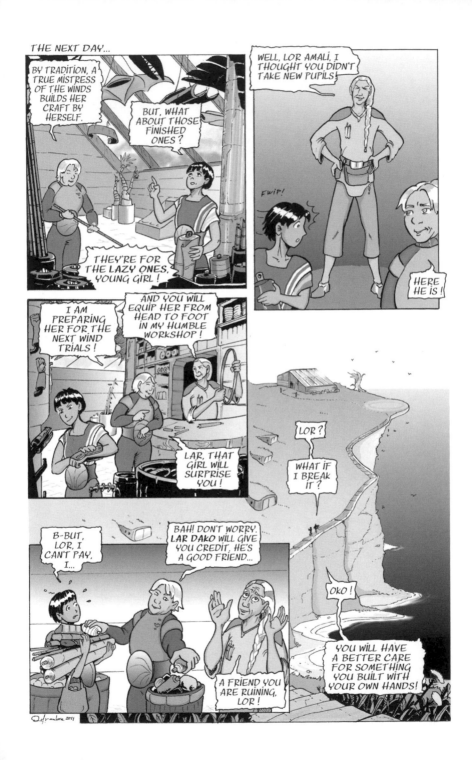

* SPIRALS: THE SOCIAL DIVISIONS OF A CITY, FROM THE HILL'S SUMMIT TO THE BASE

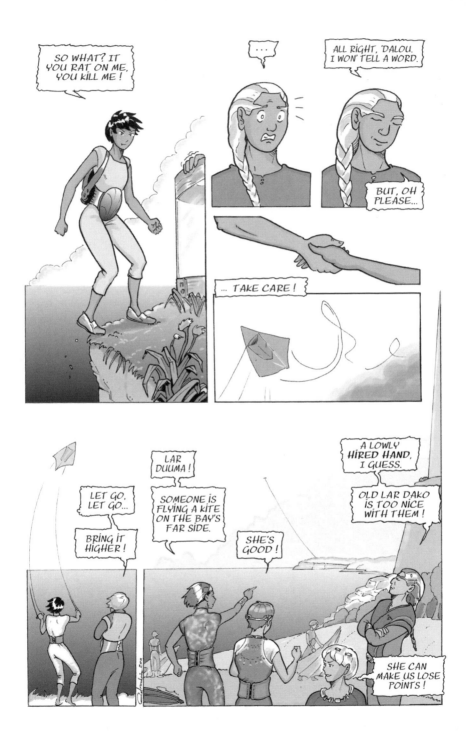

PART THREE

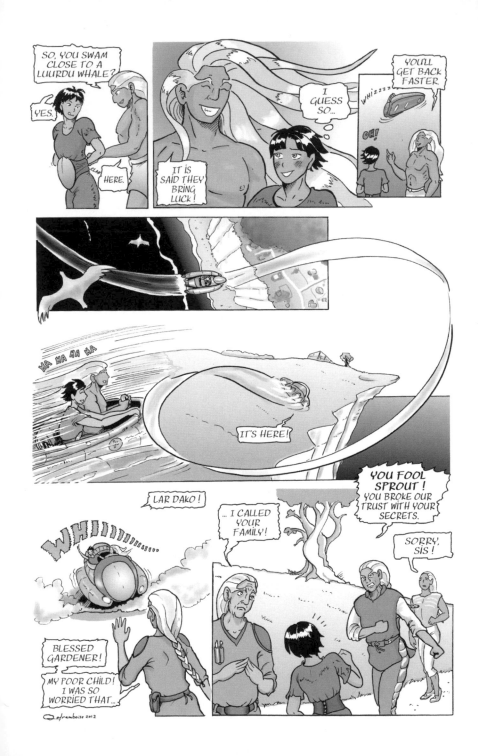

* MUNICIPAL CONCILLOR

PART FOUR

The End

AMONG THE GARDENERS

THE BOTA TREE

GIVES FLOWERS, SEEDS, EDIBLE FRUITS. ITS BARK FIBER WAS USED TO WEAVE NETS AND CLOTHES.

THE BOTA IS PLANTED AND VENERATED ON EVERY WORLD, BECAUSE IT OFFERED A VITAL REFUGE FOR THE GARDENERS' EARLY ANCESTORS.

IT IS A SYMBOL OF GENEROSITY

THE CHILDREN'S BRANCH. (THERE'S ALWAYS ONE.)

ADALOU'S OPINION...

YOU CAN'T BEAT MODERN CUMFORT!

THE NEIGHBORS ARE NOISY TONIGHT.

GOOD THING WE MOVED TO A HIGH PLACE.

iik-iik-ik
CRUNCH
ROARR
GRRRR
SSSSSH
SNAP
KAI-OKAI-KAI-KAI
KRAK

HIRED-HANDS

THE HIRED-HANDS OF BOTH SEXES EXECUTE EXHAUSTING TASKS TO PAY OFF THEIR DEBT.

LIKE WEEDING THE RICH'S GARDENS.

WOMEN WEAR A RUDIMENTARY SHIELD WOVEN FROM REEDS.

loose

tight

THEY MUST REPLACE IT AS SOON AS THE KNOTS LOOSEN!

UNKEMPT HAIR, NO INSIGNIAS

WOO-HOO! CHECK THOSE SOFT BELLIES!

BRAINLESS WIGS!

oOOH!

NOT QUITE HONEST

YOUNG MEN OFTEN EXHIBIT VULGARITY

SOME ARE APT TO COMMIT PETTY THEFTS OF INSIGNIAS

WILD SEEDS!

OUCH!

HSS HSS HSS

HSS HSS

WE'LL DRINK A CASK OF BOURBI TONIGHT!

THE SOCIAL LADDER AT LUDALLAH

THE UMBRELLA

THE UMBRELLA IS AN A.I. LINKED TO A CITY, THAT
COMPUTE THE PRESTIGE LEVELS OF EACH CITIZEN
AND EACH HOUSEHOLD.

THE UMBRELLA
UNDER ITS MOBILE
FORM.

THE A.I. CHANNELS ALL COMMUNICATIONS AND
ECONOMICAL EXCHANGES BETWEEN CITIES.
IT ASSISTS THE PRAEFECT IN RESOLUTION OF
DISPUTES AND THE PRESTIGE ACCOUNT.

ITS HEART IS WELL BURIED UNDER THE TOWER'S BASE,
SO IT IS PROTECTED AGAINST ELECTROMAGNETIC DISCHARGES.
ITS ROOT NET CIRCULATES UNDERGROUND. THE CITIZENS
CONSULT THE SURFACE INTERACTIVE TERMINALS.

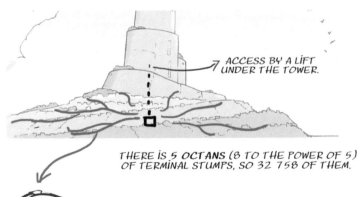

ACCESS BY A LIFT
UNDER THE TOWER.

THERE IS 5 OCTANS (8 TO THE POWER OF 5)
OF TERMINAL STUMPS, SO 32 758 OF THEM.

ONE INTERACTIVE UMBRELLA TERMINAL

THEY TRANSMIT ALL INFORMATIONS
FROM THE CITY'S INTELLIGENCE.
THEY CAN BE FOUND IN HOUSES
AS WELL AS ON THE STREETS.

THE TOWER

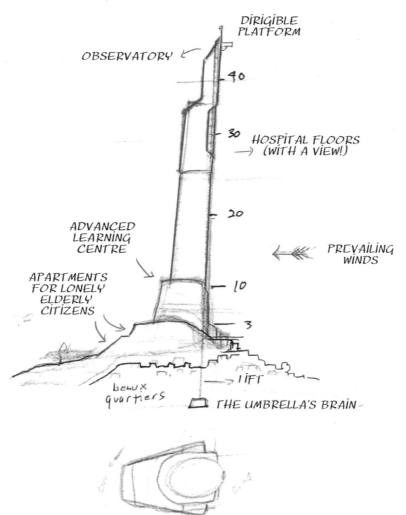

DIRIGIBLE PLATFORM

OBSERVATORY

40

30 HOSPITAL FLOORS → (WITH A VIEW!)

20

ADVANCED LEARNING CENTRE

APARTMENTS FOR LONELY ELDERLY CITIZENS

10

← PREVAILING WINDS

3

beaux quartiers

LIFT

THE UMBRELLA'S BRAIN

THE TOWER IS THE BEATING HEART OF THE CITY,
CUMULATING THE FONCTIONS OF AN HOSPITAL,
HIGHER EDUCATION CENTER, AND RESEARCH.

AT ITS SUMMIT, A COMMUNICATION
CENTER AND THE DIRIGIBLE PLATFORM.

AT ITS BASE, ARE APPARTMENTS RESERVED
FOR RETIRED CITIZEN WHO HAVE NO FAMILY.
SO THEY LIVE CLOSE TO THE CARE THEY NEED.

THE CLIFF "SMILES"

THE SMILES ARE VENOMOUS MOLLUSKS STUCK ON THE CLIFF THAT ATTRACT FLIES WITH THE SWEET WAX COVERING THEIR SHELL. THOSE INSECTS IN TURN DRAW THE SHORE BIRDS, THAT ARE THE VERITABLE PREYS OF THE SMILES.

THEIR VENOM IS RARELY FATAL TO ADULT GARDENERS, BUT THEY STILL CAN BE PARALYSED AND LATER DROWN WHEN THE TIDE RISES.

ORIGINS

The Gardeners (Chh'atyls: the people sprouted from the ground, in their language) arc humanoids whose evolution followed a different path than humans. Their skin does some photosynthesis, which provides them with energy to supplement their food. (Their meals include very little sugar. Only the elderly or sick need to eat sweet foods).

A genetic hiccup, women develop a sift belly, from the weakening of the abdominal muscles to let the daylight pass to the fetus. They must wear a protective shield, while the young men proudly display their abs.

Hair is a source of pride (and rivalry!) among men who wear it long. It is not uncommon to see boys pulling each other's braids during fights.

Accumulated merit is the basis of the social system, calculated in prestige points, and steps on the Honor Stairway. But, like in any society, corruption and power are concentrated in the upper classes.

All worship Chhoani, the Great Gardener, creator of the universe, his daughter Silene the Sower, her mischievous half-brother Koudriss and, finally, the Lazy Gardener in love with Silene.

The sketches on the following pages complete this very short visit. For more information, see the series of novels.

∿

LEXICON

- Bota: the most revered tree in the Empire.
- Bourbi: a small fruit giving a great liquor
- Chhoani: the great Gardener who created the universe.
- Chh'atyl : the people sprouted off the ground.
- Kho, kha : filiation link
- Koudriss: crafty half-brother of Silène
- Krel: time unit, contains 64 pikrels
- Lazy Gardener : Silène's legendary lover
- Lar, Lor : (spouse) equiv. of mister, misses
- Ludallah : «green hill», Luurdu's capital.
- Luurdu: a tropical climate planet
- Nuibine : a red funnel-shaped flower
- Octan: power of eight (two octans: 64).
- Oko!: Expression of disagreement, forceful no!
- Little sun: the dandelion, scattered everywhere
- Pikrel: one 64e of a krel, about one and a half minute
- Silène la Semeuse: daughter of Chhoani
- Siouye : distance unit, about 600 m
- Tac!: expression of agreement

SKETCHES

A LUURDU "WHALE"

AN AQUATIC CREATURE SOMETIMES MIGRATING
AROUND THE COASTS (AND FORTUNATELY UNEDIBLE).
IT IS SAID THAT SEEING ONE BRINGS GOOD LUCK.

(BLUE PENCIL ON BRISTOL PAPER)

ADALOU KHA NARRI

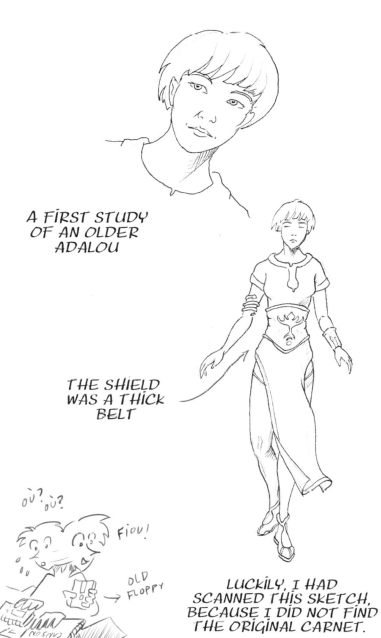

A FIRST STUDY
OF AN OLDER
ADALOU

THE SHIELD
WAS A THICK
BELT

OÙ? OÙ?

FIOU!

OLD FLOPPY

LUCKILY, I HAD
SCANNED THIS SKETCH,
BECAUSE I DID NOT FIND
THE ORIGINAL CARNET.

FACES STUDIES

Narri. Adolou Amali Daku père hostile frère rivale

THUMBNAIL OF
LAR DAKO'S
WORKSHOP PAGE

LAR DAKO

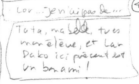

LAR DAKO IS A FINE
CHARACTER WHO APPEARS
IN THE 5TH NOVEL OF
THE CHAAAS SERIES.

ADALOU'S FAMILY HOUSE CONCEPT

TWO STORIES,
LINKED BY A CENTRAL STAIR

READING PLATES
ON THE WALL

WATER BASIN

STUDY
SADDLE

ADALOU'S ROOM - WITH THE BASKET-BED.

THE TOWER AND LUDALLAH CITY

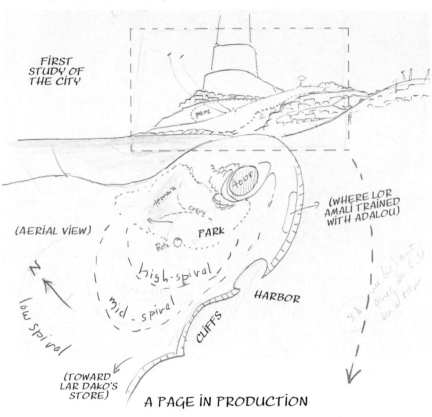

FIRST STUDY OF THE CITY

(AERIAL VIEW)

park

tour

terrain

creux

Bois O.

PARK

high-spiral

mid-spiral

low spiral

N

(WHERE LOR AMALI TRAINED WITH ADALOU)

HARBOR

CLIFFS

(TOWARD LAR DAKO'S STORE)

A PAGE IN PRODUCTION

KITE GUIDING GEAR

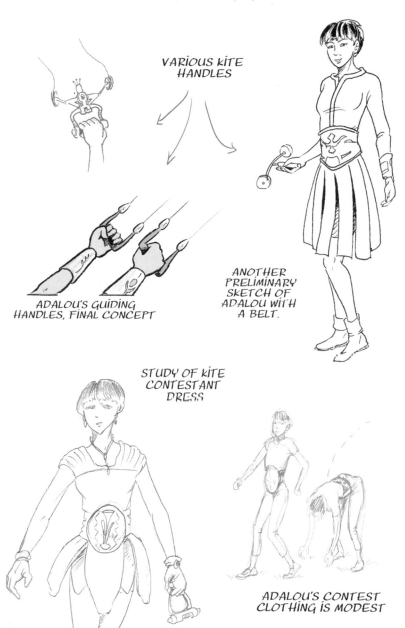

VARIOUS KITE HANDLES

ADALOU'S GUIDING HANDLES, FINAL CONCEPT

ANOTHER PRELIMINARY SKETCH OF ADALOU WITH A BELT.

STUDY OF KITE CONTESTANT DRESS

ADALOU'S CONTEST CLOTHING IS MODEST

PRODUCTION STEPS

FOR ONE PANEL

PENCILLING	INKING	POST-TREATMENT: GRAY TONES AND FONTS

TALKING TO THE WIND

Comics were my first love before I decided to write stories that were too long to craft with pen and paper. But drawing is a need of the soul that comes back at me like a boomerang, as the years roll by without stopping.

Mistress of the Winds stems from my love of kites, a sport I don't practice often now, and from my science fiction series that began with *La Quête de Chaaas* (Chaaas' Quest), which follows an impulsive teenager in a civilization of super-gardeners. Chaaas will adventure and mature through five novels.

In the second novel, which takes place on an ocean planet, his path crosses that of an adult Adalou, a kite guide who displays a great mastery of her art and teaches students. I had wanted to tell her youth in this graphic novel, which also allowed me to explore, in

2011, the world I that would be featured in the fifth book of the series. This last novel takes place on Adalou's home planet, which we also meet again.

That is to say, this young girl has a bright future ahead of her.

I am grateful to my colleague and colorist Frank Fournier, who kindly designed the fonts used on the pages while I was producing the cover. And to the folks at Rapido Books, who printed the book despite the epidemic of... paper shortage!

ABOUT THE AUTHOR

Beside trying to initiate first contact with strange flora, Michèle Laframboise feeds coffee grounds to her garden plants, runs long distances and writes full-time.

Fascinated by sciences and nature since she could walk, she has published 19 novels and over 60 short-stories in French and English, earning various distinctions in Canada and Europe. She is also a comic enthusiast who drew a dozen of graphic novels and maintains an illustrated blog.

Her stories have been featured in Solaris, Galaxies, Fiction River, Compelling Science Fiction, Abyss&Apex, Future SF, Analog and Asimov's. Holding degrees in geography and engineering, she draws from her scientific background to create worlds filled with humor, invention and wonder.

Publisher's website: echofictions.com

Michele's website: michele-laframboise.com

- facebook.com/michele.laframboise
- twitter.com/savantefolle
- instagram.com/michelesff
- goodreads.com/sundayartist

OTHER BOOKS BY MICHÈLE

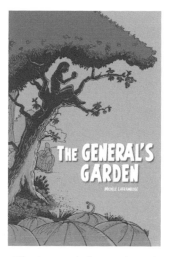

Warriors are the best gardeners !

Science-fiction / young public / alien civilisation

Chaaas and his friends break into a lush garden belonging to a retired general to steal his exotic fruits, some even hailing from the dangerous humans! But nothing is more dangerous than the general's faithful gardener...

A short comic book by Michèle Laframboise.

The General's Garden, 24 p, B&W interior art, paperback.

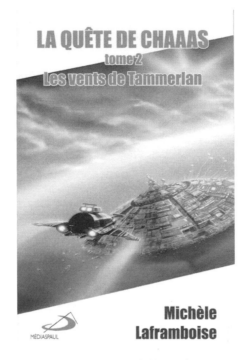

Tome 2 : Les vents de Tammerlan

Science-fiction / jeunesse / in translation

The tribulations of an adolescent growing in a space-faring, super-gardeners' civilisation – 5 short novels, an original SF series from Michèle Laframboise.

Chaaas, whose name means fire of the earth (*chaa+haas*) has an impulsive temper that often gets him in trouble, luckily balanced by his generous nature and his quest for justice. Lonely teens will find a worthy companion in this science fiction saga.

More info: michele-laframboise.com/livres/chaaas/

Otaku Ladies

Control Game

STORY & ART BY MICHÈLE LAFRAMBOISE

Saving the world, one byte at the time!

Science fiction / humor / manga

The Otaku Ladies are a trio of talented geek ladies solving (and sometimes creating!) problems in various cyber environments.

In Control Game, tensions erupt in the trio as a contract snells too fishy to accept, but they need to pay the rent don't they?

B&W, 24 pages. Sunday Artist Studio

Those titles and more are available via Echofictions.com

YEARNING FOR MORE?

Michèle Laframboise's full bibliography is enough to whet any SF reader's appetite! Explore it on her official author site at:

michele-laframboise.com

New stories are brewing up constantly !

To get exclusive offers, some free readings, advanced information on special events, join Michele's merry band of readers at :

michele-laframboise.com/fans

or visit the Echofictions.com website